Student Edition

FRUIT
~ BY THE ~
BUSHEL

ROOTED IN CHRIST FOR SPIRITUAL GROWTH

PAUL CHAPPELL

First published in 2013 by Striving Together Publications, a
ministry of Lancaster Baptist Church, Lancaster, CA 93535.
Striving Together Publications is committed to providing tried,
trusted, and proven books that will further equip local churches
to carry out the Great Commission. Your comments and
suggestions are valued.

Striving Together Publications
4020 E. Lancaster Blvd.
Lancaster, CA 93535
800.201.7748

Cover design by Andrew Hutchens
Layout by Breanna Hawkins
Special thanks to our proofreaders

The author and publication team have put forth every
effort to give proper credit to quotes and thoughts that are
not original with the author. It is not our intent to claim
originality with any quote or thought that could not readily
be tied to an original source.

ISBN 978–1-59894–226–2
Printed in the United States of America

Table of Contents

Rooted in Christ

Key Verses

Colossians 2:6–8

6   As ye have therefore received Christ Jesus the Lord, so walk ye in him:

7   Rooted and built up in him, and stablished in the faith, as ye have been taught, abounding therein with thanksgiving.

8   Beware lest any man spoil you through philosophy and vain deceit, after the tradition of men, after the rudiments of the world, and not after Christ.

Psalm 1:1–6

1   Blessed is the man that walketh not in the counsel of the ungodly, nor standeth in the way of sinners, nor sitteth in the seat of the scornful.

2   But his delight is in the law of the Lord; and in his law doth he meditate day and night.

3   And he shall be like a tree planted by the rivers of water, that bringeth forth his fruit in his season; his leaf also shall not wither; and whatsoever he doeth shall prosper.

4   The ungodly are not so: but are like the chaff which the wind driveth away.

5   Therefore the ungodly shall not stand in the judgment, nor sinners in the congregation of the righteous.

6   For the Lord knoweth the way of the righteous: but the way of the ungodly shall perish.

Overview

Rootedness in Christ is a choice. We become planted in Christ at salvation, and we must choose to let our spiritual roots sink deeply into the soil of Christ as we seek our strength, nourishment, and growth from Him.

Spiritual rootedness has enemies in the culture and the people of this world. God warns us to beware of both things and people who would try to draw us away from Christ, causing our roots to suffer.

The result of becoming firmly rooted in Christ is vibrant, consistent spiritual fruit that draws others to Him.

Introduction

_____

_____

_____

MATTHEW 13:6

6   *And when the sun was up, they were scorched; and because they had no root, they withered away.*

COLOSSIANS 2:7

7   *Rooted and built up in him, and stablished in the faith, as ye have been taught, abounding therein with thanksgiving.*

2 CORINTHIANS 11:13–14

13   *For such are false apostles, deceitful workers, transforming themselves into the apostles of Christ.*

14   *And no marvel; for Satan himself is transformed into an angel of light.*

GALATIANS 5:17

17   *For the flesh lusteth against the Spirit, and the Spirit against the flesh: and these are contrary the one to the other: so that ye cannot do the things that ye would.*

2 TIMOTHY 3:1–3

1   *This know also, that in the last days perilous times shall come.*

2   *For men shall be lovers of their own selves, covetous, boasters, proud, blasphemers, disobedient to parents, unthankful, unholy,*

3   *Without natural affection, trucebreakers, false accusers, incontinent, fierce, despisers of those that are good,*

PROVERBS 22:28
28 Remove not the ancient landmark, which thy fathers have set.

I. The _____ of Spiritual Roots

A. We must be _____ in Christ.

COLOSSIANS 2:6
6 As ye have therefore received Christ Jesus the Lord, so walk ye in him:

EPHESIANS 3:17
17 That Christ may dwell in your hearts by faith; that ye, being rooted and grounded in love,

B. We must _____ Christ.

MATTHEW 13:8
8 But other [seed] fell into good ground, and brought forth fruit, some an hundredfold, some sixtyfold, some thirtyfold.

PSALM 1:2–3
2 But his delight is in the law of the LORD; and in his law doth he meditate day and night.
3 And he shall be like a tree planted by the rivers of water, that bringeth forth his fruit in his season; his leaf also shall not wither; and whatsoever he doeth shall prosper.

ACTS 17:11

11 These were more noble than those in Thessalonica, in that they received the word with all readiness of mind, and searched the scriptures daily, whether those things were so.

1 TIMOTHY 4:7

7 But refuse profane and old wives' fables, and exercise thyself rather unto godliness.

II. The _____ of Spiritual Roots

COLOSSIANS 2:8

8 Beware lest any man spoil you through philosophy and vain deceit, after the tradition of men, after the rudiments of the world, and not after Christ.

A. The culture of this _____ is an enemy.

ROMANS 1:25

25 Who changed the truth of God into a lie, and worshipped and served the creature more than the Creator, who is blessed for ever. Amen.

2 THESSALONIANS 3:6

6 Now we command you, brethren, in the name of our Lord Jesus Christ, that ye withdraw yourselves from every brother that walketh disorderly, and not after the tradition which he received of us.

B. The crowd of the _____ **is an enemy.**

PSALM 1:1

1   Blessed is the man that walketh not in the counsel of
the ungodly, nor standeth in the way of sinners, nor sitteth
in the seat of the scornful.

III. The _____ of Spiritual Roots

A. We will produce _____ **fruit.**

GALATIANS 5:22–23

22   But the fruit of the Spirit is love, joy, peace, longsuffering,
gentleness, goodness, faith,
23   Meekness, temperance: against such there is no law.

PSALM 1:3

3   And he shall be like a tree planted by the rivers of water,
that bringeth forth his fruit in his season; his leaf also shall
not wither; and whatsoever he doeth shall prosper.

B. We will produce _____ **fruit.**

PSALM 1:4

4   The ungodly are not so: but are like the chaff which
the wind driveth away.

Conclusion

_____

_____

_____

Study Questions

1. Give examples of things that are uprooted in our culture.

2. What are two of the five reasons given at the beginning of this lesson as to why it is vital that we be rooted in Christ?

3. What three choices are indispensable in a decision to seek Christ in His Word?

4. What caused the Bereans we read about in Acts 17 to be "more noble"?

5. Many landmarks of truth are being removed from our society—landmarks such as prayer in public schools and the Ten Commandments in government buildings. What landmarks of truth are you striving to keep strong in your life and in the lives of your family members?

6. Do you recognize the two enemies of rootedness in Christ—the world's philosophy and ungodly acquaintances—warring in your life? What specific enemies of these types do you see, and what steps can you take to overcome them?

7. When there is a problem with the fruit, we should first examine the roots to see where the weakness is coming from. What are some current problems in your life, and how do you think they may be corrected if you were to deepen your roots in Christ?

8. The two surveys we spoke of point to the fact that approximately half of Americans never think about eternity and Heaven or seeking God's wisdom. How much time do you spend seeking wisdom from God and meditating on your Heavenly Father?

Memory Verse

PSALM 1:3

3   And he shall be like a tree planted by the rivers of water, that bringeth forth his fruit in his season; his leaf also shall not wither; and whatsoever he doeth shall prosper.

Rooted in Christ's Word

Key Verses

JAMES 1:19–25

19 *Wherefore, my beloved brethren, let every man be swift to hear, slow to speak, slow to wrath:*

20 *For the wrath of man worketh not the righteousness of God.*

21 *Wherefore lay apart all filthiness and superfluity of naughtiness, and receive with meekness the engrafted word, which is able to save your souls.*

22 *But be ye doers of the word, and not hearers only, deceiving your own selves.*

23 *For if any be a hearer of the word, and not a doer, he is like unto a man beholding his natural face in a glass:*

24 *For he beholdeth himself, and goeth his way, and straightway forgetteth what manner of man he was.*

25 *But whoso looketh into the perfect law of liberty, and continueth therein, he being not a forgetful hearer, but a doer of the work, this man shall be blessed in his deed.*

Overview

As both Jesus Christ and the Bible are the living Word of God, it is impossible to be rooted in Christ without being rooted in His Word. A genuine disciple of Christ prepares his or her heart to humbly receive God's Word and to allow it to be his or her guide through life.

Introduction

_____

_____

_____

JOHN 1:1
1   In the beginning was the Word, and the Word was with God, and the Word was God.

PSALM 119:140
140 Thy word is very pure: therefore thy servant loveth it.

JOHN 8:31–32
31   Then said Jesus to those Jews which believed on him, If ye continue in my word, then are ye my disciples indeed;
32   And ye shall know the truth, and the truth shall make you free.

PSALM 19:7–8
7   The law of the LORD is perfect, converting the soul: the testimony of the LORD is sure, making wise the simple.
8   The statutes of the LORD are right, rejoicing the heart: the commandment of the LORD is pure, enlightening the eyes.

I. Prepared to _____ (vv. 19–21)

A. *We need a spirit of* _____ *. (v. 19)*

PROVERBS 17:28

28 Even a fool, when he holdeth his peace, is counted wise: and he that shutteth his lips is esteemed a man of understanding.

JAMES 3:1

1 My brethren, be not many masters, knowing that we shall receive the greater condemnation.

GALATIANS 4:16

16 Am I therefore become your enemy, because I tell you the truth?

B. We need a spirit of _____ **. (v. 21)**

ACTS 17:11

11 These were more noble than those in Thessalonica, in that they received the word with all readiness of mind…

II. Planning to _____ (v. 22)

A. _____ **the Word.**

2 TIMOTHY 4:3–4

3 For the time will come when they will not endure sound doctrine; but after their own lusts shall they heap to themselves teachers, having itching ears;

4 And they shall turn away their ears from the truth, and shall be turned unto fables.

MARK 7:16

16 If any man have ears to hear, let him hear.

2 TIMOTHY 3:15
15 And that from a child thou hast known the holy scriptures...

B. _____ **the Word.**

III. Persistent in _____ (vv. 23–25)

A. _____ **the Word. (vv. 23–24)**

B. _____ **in the Word. (v. 25)**

JOSHUA 1:8
8   This book of the law shall not depart out of thy mouth; but thou shalt meditate therein day and night, that thou mayest observe to do according to all that is written therein; for then thou shalt make thy way prosperous, and then thou shalt have good success.

Conclusion

_____

_____

_____

Study Questions

1. Fill in the blanks: Wherever there is a _____ problem, there is likely a _____ problem.

2. In what verse did Jesus say that His disciples would continue in His Word?

3. What are two attitudes that prepare our hearts for the Word of God?

4. James 1:23–25 compares God's Word to what?

5. How do you prepare your heart to receive God's Word before you go to church? What changes will you make this week to enable your heart to be more receptive to the preaching and reading of the Word of God?

6.   Jesus said eight times in the gospels, "He that hath ears to hear, let him hear." What indicators do you see in your life that you have ears to hear? What indicators do you see that would prompt you to be more focused on receiving spiritual truth?

7.   God instructs us to be a *doer*, or a *performer*, of God's Word. Are you following God's script or the scripts the world places before you? What specific changes could you make that would help you to perform God's script?

8.   God instructs us to look into the mirror of God's Word and allow it to change us. Will you commit to daily looking into His Word, making the necessary changes your reflection indicates?

Memory Verse

JOSHUA 1:8
8   This book of the law shall not depart out of thy mouth; but thou shalt meditate therein day and night, that thou mayest observe to do according to all that is written therein: for then thou shalt make thy way prosperous, and then thou shalt have good success.

Rooted in Christ's Truth

Key Verses

2 JOHN 1–12

1   The elder unto the elect lady and her children, whom I love in the truth; and not I only, but also all they that have known the truth;

2   For the truth's sake, which dwelleth in us, and shall be with us for ever.

3   Grace be with you, mercy, and peace, from God the Father, and from the Lord Jesus Christ, the Son of the Father, in truth and love.

4   I rejoiced greatly that I found of thy children walking in truth, as we have received a commandment from the Father.

5   And now I beseech thee, lady, not as though I wrote a new commandment unto thee, but that which we had from the beginning, that we love one another.

6   And this is love, that we walk after his commandments. This is the commandment, That, as ye have heard from the beginning, ye should walk in it.

7   For many deceivers are entered into the world, who confess not that Jesus Christ is come in the flesh. This is a deceiver and an antichrist.

8   Look to yourselves, that we lose not those things which we have wrought, but that we receive a full reward.

9   Whosoever transgresseth, and abideth not in the doctrine of Christ, hath not God. He that abideth in the doctrine of Christ, he hath both the Father and the Son.

10   If there come any unto you, and bring not this doctrine, receive him not into your house, neither bid him God speed:

11 *For he that biddeth him God speed is partaker of his evil deeds.*

12 *Having many things to write unto you, I would not write with paper and ink: but I trust to come unto you, and speak face to face, that our joy may be full.*

Overview

Rootedness in Christ stems from a desire to grow in Him—and a decision to trust Him and His ways. We learn those ways through His Word, and those ways are rooted in His truth. Without Christ's truth, we cannot know Him.

Introduction

_____

_____

_____

JOHN 17: 17, 20
17 Sanctify them through thy truth: thy word is truth.
20 Neither pray I for these alone, but for them also which shall believe on me through their word;

I. Our _____ to the Truth (vv. 1–3)

A. It is our _____. (v. 1)

1 JOHN 4:10
10 Herein is love, not that we loved God, but that he loved us, and sent his Son to be the propitiation for our sins.

ROMANS 8:38–39
38 For I am persuaded, that neither death, nor life, nor angels, nor principalities, nor powers, nor things present, nor things to come,
39 Nor height, nor depth, nor any other creature, shall be able to separate us from the love of God, which is in Christ Jesus our Lord.

PHILIPPIANS 1:9–10
9 And this I pray, that your love may abound yet more and more in knowledge and in all judgment.

10   *That ye may approve things that are excellent; that ye may be sincere and without offence till the day of Christ.*

ACTS 2:42
42   *And they continued stedfastly in the apostles' doctrine and fellowship, and in breaking of bread, and in prayers.*

JOHN 14:6
6   *Jesus saith unto him, I am the way, the truth, and the life: no man cometh unto the Father, but by me.*

B.   It is our _____ **. (vv. 2–3)**

MALACHI 3:6
6   *For I am the LORD, I change not...*

HEBREWS 13:8
8   *Jesus Christ, the same yesterday, and to day, and forever.*

2 JOHN 3
3   *Grace be with you, mercy, and peace, from God the Father, and from the Lord Jesus Christ, the Son of the Father, in truth and love.*

II. Our _____ with the Truth (vv. 4–8)

A.   We need to _____ **. (v. 4)**

DEUTERONOMY 17:18–19
18   *And it shall be, when he sitteth upon the throne of his kingdom, that he shall write him a copy of this law in a book out of that which is before the priests the Levites:*

19 *And it shall be with him, and he shall read therein all the days of his life: that he may learn to fear the LORD his God, to keep all the words of this law and these statutes, to do them.*

2 TIMOTHY 2:15

15 *Study to shew thyself approved unto God, a workman that needeth not to be ashamed, rightly dividing the word of truth.*

PSALM 119:11, 18

11 *Thy word have I hid in mine heart, that I might not sin against thee.*

18 *Open thou mine eyes, that I may behold wondrous things out of thy law.*

1 CORINTHIANS 2:10

10 *But God hath revealed them unto us by his Spirit: for the Spirit searcheth all things, yea, the deep things of God.*

JOHN 14:26

26 *But the Comforter, which is the Holy Ghost, whom the Father will send in my name, he shall teach you all things, and bring all things to your remembrance, whatsoever I have said unto you.*

PSALM 119:9

9 *Wherewithal shall a young man cleanse his way? by taking heed thereto according to thy word.*

JAMES 1:22

22 *But be ye doers of the word, and not hearers only, deceiving your own selves.*

B. We need to _____. (vv. 5–6)

JOHN 13:34–35

34 A new commandment I give unto you, That ye love one another; as I have loved you, that ye also love one another.

35 By this shall all men know that ye are my disciples, if ye have love one to another.

C. We need to _____. (vv. 7–8)

1 PETER 5:8

8 Be sober, be vigilant; because your adversary the devil, as a roaring lion, walketh about, seeking whom he may devour.

1 JOHN 2:23

23 Whosoever denieth the Son, the same hath not the Father: (but) he that acknowledgeth the Son hath the Father also.

GALATIANS 3:1–3

1 O foolish Galatians, who hath bewitched you, that ye should not obey the truth, before whose eyes Jesus Christ hath been evidently set forth, crucified among you?

2 This only would I learn of you, Received ye the Spirit by the works of the law, or by the hearing of faith?

3 Are ye so foolish? having begun in the Spirit, are ye now made perfect by the flesh?

III. Our _____ in the Truth (vv. 9–12)

A. We have an _____ relationship. (v. 9)

JOHN 3:36

36 *He that believeth on the Son hath everlasting life: and he that believeth not the Son shall not see life; but the wrath of God abideth on him.*

ACTS 4:12

12 *Neither is there salvation in any other: for there is none other name under heaven given among men, whereby we must be saved.*

1 JOHN 5:20

20 *And we know that the Son of God is come, and hath given us an understanding, that we may know him that is true, and we are in him that is true, even in his Son Jesus Christ. This is the true God, and eternal life.*

B. We have an _____ fellowship. (vv. 10–12)

Conclusion

_____

_____

_____

Study Questions

1. What is the greatest possible danger in having a deep cultural interest?

2. How does our relationship to truth affect us eternally?

3. Name two types of bonds created through acceptance of truth.

4. What three responsibilities do we have to truth?

5. Common beliefs create common bonds. List some of your relational bonds. Are they formed more through spiritual or social beliefs?

6. Do you find yourself negotiating truth in your mind in order to not offend someone because you have a desire to minister to them? If so, what truths have you let slip and what steps could you take to recover those truths?

7. Have you made personal decisions to keep yourself grounded in Christ's truth? Which of the five decisions mentioned are already part of your life? Which ones could you add this week?

8. Colossians 2:6 encourages, "As ye have therefore received Christ Jesus the Lord, so walk ye in him." Has your relationship to Christ deepened to the point where you are walking in Him? If not, what steps can you take to deepen your roots in His truth?

Memory Verse

JOHN 14:6

6   Jesus saith unto him, I am the way, the truth, and the life: no man cometh unto the Father, but by me.

Rooted in Christ's Wisdom

Key Verses

JAMES 3:13–17

13 Who is a wise man and endued with knowledge among you? let him shew out of a good conversation his works with meekness of wisdom.

14 But if ye have bitter envying and strife in your hearts, glory not, and lie not against the truth.

15 This wisdom descendeth not from above, but is earthly, sensual, devilish.

16 For where envying and strife is, there is confusion and every evil work.

17 But the wisdom that is from above is first pure, then peaceable, gentle, and easy to be intreated, full of mercy and good fruits, without partiality, and without hypocrisy.

Overview

Godly wisdom is foundational to being rooted in Christ. Wisdom, be it worldly or godly, is what leads us to every decision we make and every direction we take, from the most seemingly insignificant to the weightiest matters. In this lesson, we will learn the differences between godly wisdom and worldly wisdom, and we will be challenged to evaluate our own lives to discern what type of wisdom we are walking in.

Introduction

_____

_____

_____

COLOSSIANS 2:8
8   *Beware lest any man spoil you through philosophy and vain deceit, after the tradition of men, after the rudiments of the world, and not after Christ.*

JAMES 1:5
5   *If any of you lack wisdom, let him ask of God, that giveth to all men liberally, and upbraideth not; and it shall be given him.*

I.   The _____ of Godly Wisdom (v. 13)

A.   It is shown in our _____ . (v. 13a)

JAMES 3:1
1   *My brethren, be not many masters, knowing that we shall receive the greater condemnation.*

DANIEL 2:28
28   *But there is a God in heaven that revealeth secrets, and maketh known to the king Nebuchadnezzar what shall be in the latter days…*

Acts 6:3

3   Wherefore, brethren, look ye out among you seven men of honest report, full of the Holy Ghost and wisdom, whom we may appoint over this business.

Philippians 1:27

27   Only let your conversation be as it becometh the gospel of Christ...

James 1:22

22   But be ye doers of the word, and not hearers only, deceiving your own selves.

B.   It is shown in our _____ . (v. 13b)

Proverbs 11:14

14   Where no counsel is, the people fall: but in the multitude of counsellors there is safety.

Romans 12:3

3   For I say, through the grace given unto me, to every man that is among you, not to think of himself more highly than he ought to think; but to think soberly, according as God hath dealt to every man the measure of faith.

1 Corinthians 4:7

7   For who maketh thee to differ from another? and what hast thou that thou didst not receive? now if thou didst receive it, why dost thou glory, as if thou hadst not received it?

1 Corinthians 1:31

31   ...He that glorieth, let him glory in the Lord.

II. The _____ of Godly Wisdom (vv. 14–16)

A. It is devalued when we are _____. (v. 14)

JAMES 1:26
26 *If any man among you seem to be religious, and bridleth not his tongue, but deceiveth his own heart, this man's religion is vain.*

B. It is devalued when we are _____. (vv. 15–16)

2 CORINTHIANS 4:4
4 *In whom the god of this world hath blinded the minds of them which believe not, lest the light of the glorious gospel of Christ, who is the image of God, should shine unto them.*

COLOSSIANS 2:8
8 *Beware lest any man spoil you through philosophy and vain deceit, after the tradition of men, after the rudiments of the world, and not after Christ.*

III. The _____ of Godly Wisdom (v. 17)

COLOSSIANS 2:3
3 *In whom are hid all the treasures of wisdom and knowledge.*

A. It is _____.

B. It is _____.

ROMANS 5:1

1 Therefore being justified by faith, we have peace with God through our Lord Jesus Christ.

PHILIPPIANS 4:6

6 Be careful for nothing; but in every thing by prayer and supplication with thanksgiving let your requests be made known unto God.

MATTHEW 5:9

9 Blessed are the peacemakers: for they shall be called the children of God.

C. It is _____.

EPHESIANS 4:31–32

31 Let all bitterness, and wrath, and anger, and clamour, and evil speaking, be put away from you, with all malice: 32 And be ye kind one to another, tenderhearted, forgiving one another, even as God for Christ's sake hath forgiven you.

D. It is _____.

COLOSSIANS 3:16

16 Let the word of Christ dwell in you richly in all wisdom; teaching and admonishing one another in psalms and hymns and spiritual songs, singing with grace in your hearts to the Lord.

E. *It is without* _____ .

1 PETER 1:22
22 Seeing ye have purified your souls in obeying the truth through the Spirit unto unfeigned love of the brethren, see that ye love one another with a pure heart fervently.

Conclusion

_____

_____

_____

PROVERBS 3:13
13 Happy is the man that findeth wisdom, and the man that getteth understanding.

Study Questions

1. What are the two types of wisdom?

2. What two aspects of our lives demonstrate that we are walking in godly wisdom?

3. Name some key indicators that a person is growing in godly wisdom.

4. What are three realms of peace that we can find in God?

5. What situation are you facing right now that you need godly wisdom for?

6. What steps are you going to take to ensure that you follow godly wisdom, rather than worldly wisdom as you make your decision?

7. Identify the type of spirit you have in various life relationships. Is it peaceable and gentle, or is it divisive and fractious?

8. Write out in your own words the scriptural differences between worldly and godly wisdom.

Memory Verse

JAMES 3:17

17 But the wisdom that is from above is first pure, then peaceable, gentle, and easy to be intreated, full of mercy and good fruits, without partiality, and without hypocrisy.

Rooted in Christ's Love

Key Verses

1 JOHN 4:7–11

7   *Beloved, let us love one another: for love is of God; and every one that loveth is born of God, and knoweth God.*

8   *He that loveth not knoweth not God; for God is love.*

9   *In this was manifested the love of God toward us, because that God sent his only begotten Son into the world, that we might live through him.*

10   *Herein is love, not that we loved God, but that he loved us, and sent his Son to be the propitiation for our sins.*

11   *Beloved, if God so loved us, we ought also to love one another.*

Overview

The world is seeking love but doesn't even know its definition. People expect feeling-based sensual or brotherly love to be lasting, when it is often short-lived and fleeting.

God's love, on the other hand, stems from who God is. It is a deep, unwavering, undying, faithful, sacrificial love. The Christian whose spiritual roots are planted deeply in Christ's love will manifest that love to the world.

Introduction

_____

_____

_____

1 John 1:5

5   *This then is the message which we have heard of him, and declare unto you, that God is light, and in him is no darkness at all.*

1 John 4:8

8   *He that loveth not knoweth not God; for God is love.*

I. The Love of God _____ (vv. 7–8)

A. *Love _____ with God. (v. 8)*

1 John 4:16, 19

16   *And we have known and believed the love that God hath to us. God is love; and he that dwelleth in love dwelleth in God, and God in him.*

19   *We love him, because he first loved us.*

Romans 3:11

11   *There is none that understandeth, there is none that seeketh after God.*

B. Love is _____ by God. (v. 7)

GALATIANS 5:22
22 But the fruit of the Spirit is love…

ROMANS 5:5
5 And hope maketh not ashamed; because the love of God is shed abroad in our hearts by the Holy Ghost which is given unto us.

EPHESIANS 4:32
32 And be ye kind one to another, tenderhearted, forgiving one another, even as God for Christ's sake hath forgiven you.

1 JOHN 4:7, 20
7 Beloved, let us love one another: for love is of God; and every one that loveth is born of God, and knoweth God.
20 If a man say, I love God, and hateth his brother, he is a liar: for he that loveth not his brother whom he hath seen, how can he love God whom he hath not seen?

ROMANS 12:18
18 If it be possible, as much as lieth in you, live peaceably with all men.

II. The Love of God _____ (vv. 9–10)

A. His love is _____. (v. 9)

JOHN 3:16

16 For God so loved the world, that he gave his only begotten Son, that whosoever believeth in him should not perish, but have everlasting life.

EPHESIANS 5:25

25 Husbands, love your wives, even as Christ also loved the church, and gave himself for it...

1 JOHN 4:10

10 Herein is love, not that we loved God, but that he loved us, and sent his Son to be the propitiation for our sins.

1 JOHN 2:2

2 And he is the propitiation for our sins: and not for ours only, but also for the sins of the whole world.

PSALM 103:12

12 As far as the east is from the west, so far hath he removed our transgressions from us.

B. His love is _____ . (v. 10)

ROMANS 8:35–39

35 Who shall separate us from the love of Christ? shall tribulation, or distress, or persecution, or famine, or nakedness, or peril, or sword?

36 As it is written, For thy sake we are killed all the day long; we are accounted as sheep for the slaughter.

37 Nay, in all these things we are more than conquerors through him that loved us.

38 For I am persuaded, that neither death, nor life, nor angels, nor principalities, nor powers, nor things present, nor things to come,

39 Nor height, nor depth, nor any other creature, shall be able to separate us from the love of God, which is in Christ Jesus our Lord.

JOHN 13:1
1   Now before the feast of the passover, when Jesus knew that his hour was come that he should depart out of this world unto the Father, having loved his own which were in the world, he loved them unto the end.

III. The Love of God (v. 11)

A. We must _____.

MARK 12:29–30
29 And Jesus answered him, The first of all the commandments is, Hear, O Israel; The Lord our God is one Lord:
30 And thou shalt love the Lord thy God with all thy heart, and with all thy soul, and with all thy mind, and with all thy strength: this is the first commandment.

B. We must _____.

MARK 12:31
31 And the second is like, namely this, Thou shalt love thy neighbour as thyself. There is none other commandment greater than these.

MATTHEW 5:23–24
23 Therefore if thou bring thy gift to the altar, and there rememberest that thy brother hath ought against thee;

*24 Leave there thy gift before the altar, and go thy way;
first be reconciled to thy brother, and then come and offer
thy gift.*

C. We must _____.

ROMANS 1:14–15

*14 I am debtor both to the Greeks, and to the Barbarians;
both to the wise, and to the unwise.*

*15 So, as much as in me is, I am ready to preach the
gospel to you that are at Rome also.*

2 CORINTHIANS 8:7–9

*7 Therefore, as ye abound in every thing, in faith, and
utterance, and knowledge, and in all diligence, and in
your love to us, see that ye abound in this grace also.*

*8 I speak not by commandment, but by occasion of
the forwardness of others, and to prove the sincerity of
your love.*

*9 For ye know the grace of our Lord Jesus Christ, that,
though he was rich, yet for your sakes he became poor,
that ye through his poverty might be rich.*

Conclusion

_____

_____

_____

Study Questions

1. First John contains two comprehensive statements about the nature of God. What are they?

2. What does 1 John 4:19 tell us about the love of God?

3. Why is it not accurate to speak of a "seeker" church?

4. What was God's ultimate manifestation of His love toward us?

5. We must view God's love through His light. Is He revealing areas of your life that you have tried to hide from Him—areas you haven't previously allowed His light to make known? If so, what are these areas?

6. God's nature is love. The fruit of His Spirit is love. How can those around you see His love through your life? What steps could you take this week to allow that love to develop further in your life?

7. God's love is manifested through giving—both to God and to others. If your love for God was based solely on your financial giving, how strong would you rate your love?

8. God has removed our sins from us "as far as the east is from the west." Are you able to give that same forgiveness to others, or do you find you are "keeping record books" of others' wrongs toward you? Who specifically do you need to forgive?

Memory Verses

1 JOHN 4:10–11

10 *Herein is love, not that we loved God, but that he loved us, and sent his Son to be the propitiation for our sins.*
11 *Beloved, if God so loved us, we ought also to love one another.*

A Rooted Family

Key Verses

PSALM 127:1–5

1 Except the LORD build the house, they labour in vain that build it: except the LORD keep the city, the watchman waketh but in vain.

2 It is vain for you to rise up early, to sit up late, to eat the bread of sorrows: for so he giveth his beloved sleep.

3 Lo, children are an heritage of the LORD: and the fruit of the womb is his reward.

4 As arrows are in the hand of a mighty man; so are children of the youth.

5 Happy is the man that hath his quiver full of them: they shall not be ashamed, but they shall speak with the enemies in the gate.

Overview

Despite the uprootedness of families in our society today, it is possible to develop a strong, fruitful family. But this will happen only if we build upon the strongest foundation of all—Jesus Christ. As the Designer and Institutor of the family, God alone is able to provide for and work in our families. If we yield our lives to Him and abide by His blueprint for the home, our families will begin producing fruit for His honor and glory.

Introduction

_____

_____

_____

I. The _____ of the Family (vv. 1–2)

A. He is the _____. (v. 1a)

GENESIS 2:18, 22–24

18 And the LORD God said, It is not good that the man should be alone; I will make him an help meet for him.

22 And the rib, which the LORD God had taken from man, made he a woman, and brought her unto the man.

23 And Adam said, This is now bone of my bones, and flesh of my flesh: she shall be called Woman, because she was taken out of Man.

24 Therefore shall a man leave his father and his mother, and shall cleave unto his wife: and they shall be one flesh.

MATTHEW 19:5–6

5 And said, For this cause shall a man leave father and mother, and shall cleave to his wife: and they twain shall be one flesh?

6 Wherefore they are no more twain, but one flesh. What therefore God hath joined together, let not man put asunder.

B. He is the _____. (v. 1b)

MATTHEW 7:24–27

24 *Therefore whosoever heareth these sayings of mine, and doeth them, I will liken him unto a wise man, which built his house upon a rock:*

25 *And the rain descended, and the floods came, and the winds blew, and beat upon that house; and it fell not: for it was founded upon a rock.*

26 *And every one that heareth these sayings of mine, and doeth them not, shall be likened unto a foolish man, which built his house upon the sand:*

27 *And the rain descended, and the floods came, and the winds blew, and beat upon that house; and it fell: and great was the fall of it.*

C. He is the _____. (v. 2a)

PSALM 121:4–8

4 *Behold, he that keepeth Israel shall neither slumber nor sleep.*

5 *The LORD is thy keeper: the LORD is thy shade upon thy right hand.*

6 *The sun shall not smite thee by day, nor the moon by night.*

7 *The LORD shall preserve thee from all evil: he shall preserve thy soul.*

8 *The LORD shall preserve thy going out and thy coming in from this time forth, and even for evermore.*

PROVERBS 4:23

23 *Keep thy heart with all diligence; for out of it are the issues of life.*

D. He is the _____ **. (v. 2b)**

PSALM 4:8

8 *I will both lay me down in peace, and sleep: for thou,*
LORD, only makest me dwell in safety.

HAGGAI 1:6

6 *Ye have sown much, and bring in little; ye eat, but ye*
have not enough; ye drink, but ye are not filled with drink;
ye clothe you, but there is none warm; and he that earneth
wages earneth wages to put it into a bag with holes.

II. The _____ of the Family (v. 3)

GENESIS 20:18

18 *For the LORD had fast closed up all the wombs of the house*
of Abimelech, because of Sarah Abraham's wife.

GENESIS 29:31

31 *And when the LORD saw that Leah was hated, he opened*
her womb: but Rachel was barren.

GENESIS 30:22

22 *And God remembered Rachel, and God hearkened to her,*
and opened her womb.

1 SAMUEL 1:5–6

5 *But unto Hannah he gave a worthy portion; for he loved*
Hannah: but the LORD had shut up her womb.
6 *And her adversary also provoked her sore, for to make her*
fret, because the LORD had shut up her womb.

A. Children are the _____ of the Lord. (v. 3a)

DEUTERONOMY 6:4–9

4   Hear, O Israel: The LORD our God is one LORD:

5   And thou shalt love the LORD thy God with all thine heart, and with all thy soul, and with all thy might.

6   And these words, which I command thee this day, shall be in thine heart:

7   And thou shalt teach them diligently unto thy children, and shalt talk of them when thou sittest in thine house, and when thou walkest by the way, and when thou liest down, and when thou risest up.

8   And thou shalt bind them for a sign upon thine hand, and they shall be as frontlets between thine eyes.

9   And thou shalt write them upon the posts of thy house, and on thy gates.

2 TIMOTHY 1:5

5   When I call to remembrance the unfeigned faith that is in thee, which dwelt first in thy grandmother Lois, and thy mother Eunice; and I am persuaded that in thee also.

2 TIMOTHY 3:15

15   And that from a child thou hast known the holy scriptures, which are able to make thee wise unto salvation through faith which is in Christ Jesus.

EPHESIANS 6:4

4   And, ye fathers, provoke not your children to wrath: but bring them up in the nurture and admonition of the Lord.

B. Children are a _____ from the Lord. (v. 3b)

JEREMIAH 1:5

5   Before I formed thee in the belly I knew thee; and before thou camest forth out of the womb I sanctified thee, and I ordained thee a prophet unto the nations.

LUKE 2:5

5   To be taxed with Mary his espoused wife, being great with child.

PSALM 139:13–15

13   For thou hast possessed my reins: thou hast covered me in my mother's womb.

14   I will praise thee; for I am fearfully and wonderfully made: marvellous are thy works; and that my soul knoweth right well.

15   My substance was not hid from thee, when I was made in secret, and curiously wrought in the lowest parts of the earth.

III. The _____ of the Family (vv. 4–5)

A. _____ is needed. (vv. 4–5a)

PROVERBS 22:6

6   Train up a child in the way he should go: and when he is old, he will not depart from it.

PROVERBS 4:1–2

1   *Hear, ye children, the instruction of a father, and attend to know understanding.*

2   *For I give you good doctrine, forsake ye not my law.*

B. _____ *is provided. (v. 5b)*

Conclusion

_____

_____

_____

PSALM 68:6

6   *God setteth the solitary in families…*

JAMES 4:6

6   *But he giveth more grace. Wherefore he saith, God resisteth the proud, but giveth grace unto the humble.*

Study Questions

1. What are two Scripture references which tell us that God ordained and instituted the family?

2. In Psalm 127:1, what does the word *keep* refer to? In what ways does God keep our families?

3. What examples in Scripture remind us of God's sovereignty in providing children to families?

4. What analogy is used in Psalm 127:4–5 to demonstrate the potential of children who have been trained up in the knowledge of God?

5. What are some ways in which we can build our own homes on a biblical foundation?

6. How much time do you personally dedicate to strengthening your family? How would you say this compares to the amount of time spent in media, entertainment, hobbies, etc.?

7. Psalm 127:3 says children are a "heritage of the Lord." How often do we thank God for our children or demonstrate our thankfulness for them? How can we show our gratefulness this week?

8. A rooted family will always be strongest when its members are routinely in God's Word and presence. Are there any special blessings or needs in your life or in the life of one of your loved ones that you could bring to God as a family this week?

Memory Verse

PSALM 127:1

1 Except the LORD build the house, they labour in vain that build it: except the LORD keep the city, the watchman waketh but in vain.

A Rooted Church

Key Verses

EPHESIANS 4:11–15

11 *And he gave some, apostles; and some, prophets; and some, evangelists; and some, pastors and teachers;*

12 *For the perfecting of the saints, for the work of the ministry, for the edifying of the body of Christ:*

13 *Till we all come in the unity of the faith, and of the knowledge of the Son of God, unto a perfect man, unto the measure of the stature of the fulness of Christ:*

14 *That we henceforth be no more children, tossed to and fro, and carried about with every wind of doctrine, by the sleight of men, and cunning craftiness, whereby they lie in wait to deceive;*

15 *But speaking the truth in love, may grow up into him in all things, which is the head, even Christ:*

Overview

We have seen that rootedness in Christ is personal. It requires believers to sink their spiritual roots deeply into Christ through His Word, His truth, His wisdom, and His love. These roots require an individual walk with Christ.

We have also examined God's plan for rootedness in our families—we build and are built up in Christ through our families.

In this week's lesson, we will look at yet another means through which God brings us to maturity in Him. The local church is an indispensable tool God uses not only to build us up individually as rooted Christians, but also to enable us to build up fellow believers.

Introduction

_____

_____

_____

2 Peter 3:18
18 But grow in grace, and in the knowledge of our Lord and Saviour Jesus Christ. To him be glory both now and for ever. Amen.

I. The _____ of Growth (vv. 11–12)

A. We must _____ God's _____.
(v. 11)

Acts 1:21–22
21 Wherefore of these men which have companied with us all the time that the Lord Jesus went in and out among us,
22 Beginning from the baptism of John, unto that same day that he was taken up from us, must one be ordained to be a witness with us of his resurrection.

Acts 2:42
42 And they continued stedfastly in the apostles' doctrine and fellowship, and in breaking of bread, and in prayers.

Ephesians 2:20
20 And are built upon the foundation of the apostles and prophets, Jesus Christ himself being the chief corner stone;

ACTS 1:1–2

1   *The former treatise have I made, O Theophilus, of all that Jesus began both to do and teach,*

2   *Until the day in which he was taken up, after that he through the Holy Ghost had given commandments unto the apostles whom he had chosen:*

2 PETER 1:19–21

19   *We have also a more sure word of prophecy; whereunto ye do well that ye take heed, as unto a light that shineth in a dark place, until the day dawn, and the day star arise in your hearts:*

20   *Knowing this first, that no prophecy of the scripture is of any private interpretation.*

21   *For the prophecy came not in old time by the will of man: but holy men of God spake as they were moved by the Holy Ghost.*

ACTS 20:28–29

28   *Take heed therefore unto yourselves, and to all the flock, over the which the Holy Ghost hath made you overseers, to feed the church of God, which he hath purchased with his own blood.*

29   *For I know this, that after my departing shall grievous wolves enter in among you, not sparing the flock.*

B.   We must _____ in God's _____.
(v. 12)

EPHESIANS 4:1

1   *I therefore, the prisoner of the Lord, beseech you that ye walk worthy of the vocation wherewith ye are called,*

2 Timothy 2:2

2   And the things that thou hast heard of me among
many witnesses, the same commit thou to faithful men,
who shall be able to teach others also.

1 Thessalonians 1:3

3   Remembering without ceasing your work of faith,
and labour of love, and patience of hope in our Lord Jesus
Christ, in the sight of God and our Father;

II. The _____ of Growth (v. 13)

A. *We must have* _____ .
(v. 13a)

Jude 3

3   Beloved, when I gave all diligence to write unto you of
the common salvation, it was needful for me to write unto
you, and exhort you that ye should earnestly contend for
the faith which was once delivered unto the saints.

Philippians 1:27

27   Only let your conversation be as it becometh the
gospel of Christ: that whether I come and see you, or else
be absent, I may hear of your affairs, that ye stand fast in
one spirit, with one mind striving together for the faith of
the gospel;

2 Timothy 3:16–17

16   All scripture is given by inspiration of God, and is
profitable for doctrine, for reproof, for correction, for
instruction in righteousness:

17 That the man of God may be perfect, throughly furnished unto all good works.

B. We must have the _____. (v. 13b)

COLOSSIANS 2:2

2 That their hearts might be comforted, being knit together in love, and unto all riches of the full assurance of understanding, to the acknowledgement of the mystery of God, and of the Father, and of Christ;

ACTS 4:12

12 Neither is there salvation in any other: for there is none other name under heaven given among men, whereby we must be saved.

III. The _____ of Growth (vv. 14–15)

A. We grow through _____. (v. 14a)

1 CORINTHIANS 14:20

20 Brethren, be not children in understanding: howbeit in malice be ye children, but in understanding be men.

1 JOHN 2:19

19 They went out from us, but they were not of us; for if they had been of us, they would no doubt have continued with us: but they went out, that they might be made manifest that they were not all of us.

B. We grow through _____.
(v. 14b)

2 PETER 2:1–2

1 But there were false prophets also among the people, even as there shall be false teachers among you, who privily shall bring in damnable heresies, even denying the Lord that bought them, and bring upon themselves swift destruction.

2 And many shall follow their pernicious ways; by reason of whom the way of truth shall be evil spoken of.

1 JOHN 4:1–3

1 Beloved, believe not every spirit, but try the spirits whether they are of God: because many false prophets are gone out into the world.

2 Hereby know ye the Spirit of God: Every spirit that confesseth that Jesus Christ is come in the flesh is of God:

3 And every spirit that confesseth not that Jesus Christ is come in the flesh is not of God: and this is that spirit of antichrist, whereof ye have heard that it should come; and even now already is it in the world.

C. We grow through _____.
(v. 15)

1 CORINTHIANS 15:1

1 Moreover, brethren, I declare unto you the gospel which I preached unto you, which also ye have received, and wherein ye stand;

2 THESSALONIANS 2:15

15 Therefore, brethren, stand fast, and hold the traditions which ye have been taught, whether by word, or our epistle.

Conclusion

Study Questions

1. Through what method did God direct Paul to start local New Testament churches?

2. In the book of Ephesians, what did Paul tell the Christians would be the result of hearing and applying the Word of God to their lives?

3. Although a church may have many programs and activities, what three elements of its central focus do we find in Ephesians 4:12?

4. What two aspects does Ephesians 4:13 list that are essential elements of truth?

5. What vital kind of growth does the church help us maintain?

6. The pastor is to oversee and feed the flock of the local church. Are you at church for every service so that you can get the spiritual nourishment and direction you need? If not, will you commit to faithfulness so that you can grow stronger roots in Christ?

7. What are you doing (or will begin to do this week) spiritually to become equipped for the vocation, or calling, of the Christian life?

8. The local church is a place for building up and edifying one another. What have you done this week to build up a fellow church member? What one specific activity (that you don't presently do) will you commit to do this week to build up someone in your local church?

Memory Verse

EPHESIANS 4:13
13 Till we all come in the unity of the faith, and of the knowledge of the Son of God, unto a perfect man, unto the measure of the stature of the fulness of Christ:

Fruits of the Resurrection

Key Verses

1 CORINTHIANS 15:20–26

20 But now is Christ risen from the dead, and become the firstfruits of them that slept.

21 For since by man came death, by man came also the resurrection of the dead.

22 For as in Adam all die, even so in Christ shall all be made alive.

23 But every man in his own order: Christ the firstfruits; afterward they that are Christ's at his coming.

24 Then cometh the end, when he shall have delivered up the kingdom to God, even the Father; when he shall have put down all rule and all authority and power.

25 For he must reign, till he hath put all enemies under his feet.

26 The last enemy that shall be destroyed is death.

Overview

Rootedness in Christ brings about an expected end—fruit! As we plant our roots deeply into the nourishing soil of Christ and His Word, it is important that we understand what He has done that gives us the power to produce fruit. In this lesson, we will examine and rejoice in His resurrection—for it is Christ's resurrection that makes Him the firstfruits, giving us the power to live eternally, to grow spiritually, and to produce fruit.

Introduction

_____

_____

_____

1 Corinthians 15:4–8, 12

4   And that he was buried, and that he rose again the third day according to the scriptures:

5   And that he was seen of Cephas, then of the twelve:

6   After that, he was seen of above five hundred brethren at once; of whom the greater part remain unto this present, but some are fallen asleep.

7   After that, he was seen of James; then of all the apostles.

8   And last of all he was seen of me also, as of one born out of due time.

12   Now if Christ be preached that he rose from the dead, how say some among you that there is no resurrection of the dead?

I.   The _____ of the Resurrection (v. 20)

A. *The proof of His* _____ *(v. 20a)*

Acts 2:29–32

29   Men and brethren, let me freely speak unto you of the patriarch David, that he is both dead and buried, and his sepulchre is with us unto this day.

30 Therefore being a prophet, and knowing that God had sworn with an oath to him, that of the fruit of his loins, according to the flesh, he would raise up Christ to sit on his throne;

31 He seeing this before spake of the resurrection of Christ, that his soul was not left in hell, neither his flesh did see corruption.

32 This Jesus hath God raised up, whereof we all are witnesses.

B. The proof of His _____ (v. 20b)

ACTS 26:23

23 That Christ should suffer, and that he should be the first that should rise from the dead, and should shew light unto the people, and to the Gentiles.

1 PETER 1:3–5

3 Blessed be the God and Father of our Lord Jesus Christ, which according to his abundant mercy hath begotten us again unto a lively hope by the resurrection of Jesus Christ from the dead,

4 To an inheritance incorruptible, and undefiled, and that fadeth not away, reserved in heaven for you,

5 Who are kept by the power of God through faith unto salvation ready to be revealed in the last time.

EPHESIANS 1:13

13 In whom ye also trusted, after that ye heard the word of truth, the gospel of your salvation: in whom also after that ye believed, ye were sealed with that holy Spirit of promise,

II. The _____ of the Resurrection (vv. 21–22)

A. *The picture of* _____ *(vv. 21–22a)*

ROMANS 5:12

12 *Wherefore, as by one man sin entered into the world, and death by sin; and so death passed upon all men, for that all have sinned:*

1 CORINTHIANS 15:22

22 *For as in Adam all die…*

ROMANS 6:23

23 *For the wages of sin is death; but the gift of God is eternal life through Jesus Christ our Lord.*

B. *The picture of* _____ *(v. 22)*

ROMANS 6:11

11 *Likewise reckon ye also yourselves to be dead indeed unto sin, but alive unto God through Jesus Christ our Lord.*

1 CORINTHIANS 15:55–57

55 *O death, where is thy sting? O grave, where is thy victory?*

56 *The sting of death is sin; and the strength of sin is the law.*

57 *But thanks be to God, which giveth us the victory through our Lord Jesus Christ.*

ROMANS 1:16

16 For I am not ashamed of the gospel of Christ: for it is the power of God unto salvation to every one that believeth; to the Jew first, and also to the Greek.

III. The _____ of the Resurrection (vv. 23–26)

A. *The promise of His _____ (v. 23)*

MATTHEW 27:50–53

50 Jesus, when he had cried again with a loud voice, yielded up the ghost.

51 And, behold, the veil of the temple was rent in twain from the top to the bottom; and the earth did quake, and the rocks rent;

52 And the graves were opened; and many bodies of the saints which slept arose,

53 And came out of the graves after his resurrection, and went into the holy city, and appeared unto many.

1 CORINTHIANS 15:51–54

51 Behold, I shew you a mystery; We shall not all sleep, but we shall all be changed,

52 In a moment, in the twinkling of an eye, at the last trump: for the trumpet shall sound, and the dead shall be raised incorruptible, and we shall be changed.

53 For this corruptible must put on incorruption, and this mortal must put on immortality.

54 So when this corruptible shall have put on incorruption, and this mortal shall have put on immortality, then shall

be brought to pass the saying that is written, Death is swallowed up in victory.

1 THESSALONIANS 4:13–16

13 But I would not have you to be ignorant, brethren, concerning them which are asleep, that ye sorrow not, even as others which have no hope.

14 For if we believe that Jesus died and rose again, even so them also which sleep in Jesus will God bring with him.

15 For this we say unto you by the word of the Lord, that we which are alive and remain unto the coming of the Lord shall not prevent them which are asleep.

16 For the Lord himself shall descend from heaven with a shout, with the voice of the archangel, and with the trump of God: and the dead in Christ shall rise first:

1 THESSALONIANS 4:17

17 Then we which are alive and remain shall be caught up together with them in the clouds, to meet the Lord in the air: and so shall we ever be with the Lord.

TITUS 2:13

13 Looking for that blessed hope, and the glorious appearing of the great God and our Saviour Jesus Christ;

B. *The promise of His* _____
   (vv. 24–26)

REVELATION 19:16

16 And he hath on his vesture and on his thigh a name written, KING OF KINGS, AND LORD OF LORDS.

REVELATION 17:14

14   These shall make war with the Lamb, and the Lamb shall overcome them: for he is Lord of lords, and King of kings: and they that are with him are called, and chosen, and faithful.

1 TIMOTHY 6:14–16

14   That thou keep this commandment without spot, unrebukeable, until the appearing of our Lord Jesus Christ:
15   Which in his times he shall shew, who is the blessed and only Potentate, the King of kings, and Lord of lords;
16   Who only hath immortality, dwelling in the light which no man can approach unto; whom no man hath seen, nor can see: to whom be honour and power everlasting. Amen.

Conclusion

_____

_____

_____

2 PETER 3:11–12

11   Seeing then that all these things shall be dissolved, what manner of persons ought ye to be in all holy conversation and godliness,
12   Looking for and hasting unto the coming of the day of God, wherein the heavens being on fire shall be dissolved, and the elements shall melt with fervent heat?

Study Questions

1. What are the two areas of Christian fruit?

2. First Corinthians 15 delineates several foundational aspects of the Christian life that would be drastically different if Christ had not risen from the dead. Name at least three of them.

3. The resurrection proves Christ's power over death. Name two other truths proven by the resurrection.

4. The resurrection pictures what two aspects of our lives?

5. What was different about Christ's resurrection than other resurrections, such as Lazareth's, that makes Him the firstfruits of the resurrection?

6. Take a few moments to write out your salvation testimony and thank God for the power of His resurrection that delivered you from the curse of sin and made you alive in Christ.

7. What changes would you make in your life this week if you lived in the realization that Jesus could return at any moment? Since He is coming back, what commitments will you actually make in light of His return—in attitudes, thoughts, relationships, actions, and habits?

8. Have you thanked Christ specifically for His resurrection? Review this lesson, and jot down the various aspects of His resurrection that have made a transformation in your life.

Memory Verses

1 CORINTHIANS 15:20–21

20 But now is Christ risen from the dead, and become the firstfruits of them that slept.
21 For since by man came death, by man came also the resurrection of the dead.

Fruits of Our Witness

Key Verses

MATTHEW 28:16–20

16 *Then the eleven disciples went away into Galilee, into a mountain where Jesus had appointed them.*

17 *And when they saw him, they worshipped him: but some doubted.*

18 *And Jesus came and spake unto them, saying, All power is given unto me in heaven and in earth.*

19 *Go ye therefore, and teach all nations, baptizing them in the name of the Father, and of the Son, and of the Holy Ghost:*

20 *Teaching them to observe all things whatsoever I have commanded you: and, lo, I am with you alway, even unto the end of the world. Amen.*

Overview

During the forty days Jesus walked on earth between His resurrection and His ascension to Heaven, He gave only one command that is recorded in Scripture. This command to witness stems from Christ's resurrection since He is the firstfruits. It is through obedience to this command that we are able to continue the cycle of growing and producing fruit.

Introduction

_____

_____

_____

ACTS 4:20

20 *For we cannot but speak the things which we have seen and heard.*

1 CORINTHIANS 15:6

6 *After that, he was seen of above five hundred brethren at once; of whom the greater part remain unto this present, but some are fallen asleep.*

ACTS 1:1–3

1 *The former treatise have I made, O Theophilus, of all that Jesus began both to do and teach,*

2 *Until the day in which he was taken up, after that he through the Holy Ghost had given commandments unto the apostles whom he had chosen:*

3 *To whom also he shewed himself alive after his passion by many infallible proofs, being seen of them forty days, and speaking of the things pertaining to the kingdom of God:*

I.   The _____ to the Resurrected Christ (vv. 16–17)

A.   The _____ of worship

MATTHEW 28:1, 8–9

1   In the end of the sabbath, as it began to dawn toward the first day of the week, came Mary Magdalene and the other Mary to see the sepulchre.

8   And they departed quickly from the sepulchre with fear and great joy; and did run to bring his disciples word.

9   And as they went to tell his disciples, behold, Jesus met them, saying, All hail. And they came and held him by the feet, and worshipped him.

JOHN 20:24–25, 28–29

24   But Thomas, one of the twelve, called Didymus, was not with them when Jesus came.

25   The other disciples therefore said unto him, We have seen the Lord. But he said unto them, Except I shall see in his hands the print of the nails, and put my finger into the print of the nails, and thrust my hand into his side, I will not believe.

28   And Thomas answered and said unto him, My Lord and my God.

29   Jesus saith unto him, Thomas, because thou hast seen me, thou hast believed: blessed are they that have not seen, and yet have believed.

LUKE 24:51–52

51   And it came to pass, while he blessed them, he was parted from them, and carried up into heaven.

52   And they worshipped him, and returned to Jerusalem with great joy:

B. The _____ for worship

REVELATION 4:11
11 Thou art worthy, O Lord, to receive glory and honour and power: for thou hast created all things, and for thy pleasure they are and were created.

REVELATION 5:9
9 And they sung a new song, saying, Thou art worthy to take the book, and to open the seals thereof: for thou wast slain, and hast redeemed us to God by thy blood out of every kindred, and tongue, and people, and nation;

PSALM 95:6
6 O come, let us worship and bow down: let us kneel before the LORD our maker.

JOHN 14:6
6 Jesus saith unto him, I am the way, the truth, and the life: no man cometh unto the Father, but by me.

JOHN 4:24
24 God is a Spirit: and they that worship him must worship him in spirit and in truth.

JOHN 1:14
14 And the Word was made flesh, and dwelt among us, (and we beheld his glory, the glory as of the only begotten of the Father,) full of grace and truth.

ACTS 17:6
6 And when they found them not, they drew Jason and certain brethren unto the rulers of the city, crying, These that have turned the world upside down are come hither also;

II. The _____ of the Resurrected Christ (vv. 19–20a)

A. We are commanded to _____ _____. (v. 19a)

ACTS 5:20

20 Go, stand and speak in the temple to the people all the words of this life.

B. We are commanded to _____. (v. 19b)

ACTS 8:35–38

35 Then Philip opened his mouth, and began at the same scripture, and preached unto him Jesus.

36 And as they went on their way, they came unto a certain water: and the eunuch said, See, here is water; what doth hinder me to be baptized?

37 And Philip said, If thou believest with all thine heart, thou mayest. And he answered and said, I believe that Jesus Christ is the Son of God.

38 And he commanded the chariot to stand still: and they went down both into the water, both Philip and the eunuch; and he baptized him.

C. We are commanded to _____ _____. (v. 20a)

EPHESIANS 4:11–15

11 And he gave some, apostles; and some, prophets; and some, evangelists; and some, pastors and teachers;

12 *For the perfecting of the saints, for the work of the ministry, for the edifying of the body of Christ:*

13 *Till we all come in the unity of the faith, and of the knowledge of the Son of God, unto a perfect man, unto the measure of the stature of the fulness of Christ:*

14 *That we henceforth be no more children, tossed to and fro, and carried about with every wind of doctrine, by the sleight of men, and cunning craftiness, whereby they lie in wait to deceive;*

15 *But speaking the truth in love, may grow up into him in all things, which is the head, even Christ:*

III. The _____ of the Resurrected Christ (vv. 18, 20b)

2 CORINTHIANS 3:5

5 *Not that we are sufficient of ourselves to think any thing as of ourselves; but our sufficiency is of God;*

A. *Christ promises His _____ . (v. 18)*

EPHESIANS 1:20–21

20 *Which he wrought in Christ, when he raised him from the dead, and set him at his own right hand in the heavenly places,*

21 *Far above all principality, and power, and might, and dominion, and every name that is named, not only in this world, but also in that which is to come:*

ACTS 1:8

8   *But ye shall receive power, after that the Holy Ghost is come upon you: and ye shall be witnesses unto me both in Jerusalem, and in all Judaea, and in Samaria, and unto the uttermost part of the earth.*

1 CORINTHIANS 2:1–5

1   *And I, brethren, when I came to you, came not with excellency of speech or of wisdom, declaring unto you the testimony of God.*

2   *For I determined not to know any thing among you, save Jesus Christ, and him crucified.*

3   *And I was with you in weakness, and in fear, and in much trembling.*

4   *And my speech and my preaching was not with enticing words of man's wisdom, but in demonstration of the Spirit and of power:*

5   *That your faith should not stand in the wisdom of men, but in the power of God.*

B. Christ promises His _____ .
(v. 20b)

HEBREWS 13:5–6

5   *Let your conversation be without covetousness; and be content with such things as ye have: for he hath said, I will never leave thee, nor forsake thee.*

6   *So that we may boldly say, The Lord is my helper, and I will not fear what man shall do unto me.*

Conclusion

_____

_____

_____

ACTS 1:9–11

9   And when he had spoken these things, while they beheld, he was taken up; and a cloud received him out of their sight.
10   And while they looked stedfastly toward heaven as he went up, behold, two men stood by them in white apparel;
11   Which also said, Ye men of Galilee, why stand ye gazing up into heaven? this same Jesus, which is taken up from you into heaven, shall so come in like manner as ye have seen him go into heaven.

Study Questions

1. Describe the circle of Christian growth in relation to witnessing.

2. Scripture records only one command Christ gave during the forty days He walked on earth between His resurrection and His ascension. What was that command?

3. Worship will exalt the truth of who Jesus is and will compel us to share this truth with others. But true worship is not based on emotionalism. What is it based on?

4. In the Great Commission, Christ commanded us to go and teach (make disciples), to baptize, and to teach (help new believers become established in their faith). What does the word *baptism* mean, and what does it picture?

5. We don't have the power or resources to convince hearts of their need for Christ or to rebirth a single soul. What are two resources Christ promises to provide for witnessing?

6.   When the disciples found themselves in the presence of the resurrected Christ, they worshiped Him. Often, our own failure to worship stems from busyness in our life which crowds out the time we spend in God's presence. What time will you carve out of each day this week to meet with and to worship God?

7.   We worship Christ because He is worthy of worship. Write down several attributes and actions of Christ that make Him worthy of your worship.

8.   Write down the names of three unsaved people you know. Begin praying for their salvation, and determine how you will witness to them.

Memory Verses

MATTHEW 28:19–20

19 Go ye therefore, and teach all nations, baptizing them in the name of the Father, and of the Son, and of the Holy Ghost: 20 Teaching them to observe all things whatsoever I have commanded you: and, lo, I am with you alway, even unto the end of the world. Amen.

Fruits of Repentance

Key Verses

MATTHEW 3:1–12

1   In those days came John the Baptist, preaching in the wilderness of Judaea,

2   And saying, Repent ye: for the kingdom of heaven is at hand.

3   For this is he that was spoken of by the prophet Esaias, saying, The voice of one crying in the wilderness, Prepare ye the way of the Lord, make his paths straight.

4   And the same John had his raiment of camel's hair, and a leathern girdle about his loins; and his meat was locusts and wild honey.

5   Then went out to him Jerusalem, and all Judaea, and all the region round about Jordan,

6   And were baptized of him in Jordan, confessing their sins.

7   But when he saw many of the Pharisees and Sadducees come to his baptism, he said unto them, O generation of vipers, who hath warned you to flee from the wrath to come?

8   Bring forth therefore fruits meet for repentance:

9   And think not to say within yourselves, We have Abraham to our father: for I say unto you, that God is able of these stones to raise up children unto Abraham.

10   And now also the axe is laid unto the root of the trees: therefore every tree which bringeth not forth good fruit is hewn down, and cast into the fire.

11   I indeed baptize you with water unto repentance: but he that cometh after me is mightier than I, whose shoes I am not worthy to bear: he shall baptize you with the Holy Ghost, and with fire:

12 Whose fan is in his hand, and he will throughly purge his floor, and gather his wheat into the garner; but he will burn up the chaff with unquenchable fire.

Overview

The message of one of the most powerful preachers in the Bible was not only to teach about repentance, but also to show repentance. Structured around this man and his message, we are going to learn about the fruit of repentance. We will examine the why's and how's of repentance— what it means and why John the Baptist emphasized this particular fruit as being necessary in the lives of those who would turn to Christ.

Introduction

_____

_____

_____

GALATIANS 5:22–24
22 But the fruit of the Spirit is love, joy, peace, longsuffering, gentleness, goodness, faith,
23 Meekness, temperance: against such there is no law.
24 And they that are Christ's have crucified the flesh with the affections and lusts.

MALACHI 3:1
1   Behold, I will send my messenger, and he shall prepare the way before me: and the Lord, whom ye seek, shall suddenly come to his temple, even the messenger of the covenant, whom ye delight in: behold, he shall come, saith the LORD of hosts.

JOHN 1:6
6   There was a man sent from God, whose name was John.

MATTHEW 11:11
11 Verily I say unto you, Among them that are born of women there hath not risen a greater than John the Baptist: notwithstanding he that is least in the kingdom of heaven is greater than he.

LUKE 1:80
80 And the child grew, and waxed strong in spirit, and was in the deserts till the day of his shewing unto Israel.

I. A Unique _____ (vv. 1–3)

A. It was a _____ message. (vv. 1–2)

2 CORINTHIANS 7:10

10 For godly sorrow worketh repentance to salvation not to be repented of: but the sorrow of the world worketh death.

B. It was a _____ message. (v. 3)

MATTHEW 17:10–13

10 And his disciples asked him, saying, Why then say the scribes that Elias must first come?

11 And Jesus answered and said unto them, Elias truly shall first come, and restore all things.

12 But I say unto you, That Elias is come already, and they knew him not, but have done unto him whatsoever they listed. Likewise shall also the Son of man suffer of them.

13 Then the disciples understood that he spake unto them of John the Baptist.

ACTS 7:51–52

51 Ye stiffnecked and uncircumcised in heart and ears, ye do always resist the Holy Ghost: as your fathers did, so do ye.

52 Which of the prophets have not your fathers persecuted? and they have slain them which shewed before of the coming of the Just One; of whom ye have been now the betrayers and murderers:

II. A Unique _____ (vv. 4–6)

A. *He was a* _____ . *(v. 4)*

MATTHEW 11:8

8   But what went ye out for to see? A man clothed in soft raiment? behold, they that wear soft clothing are in kings' houses.

JOHN 1:22–23

22   Then said they unto him, Who art thou? that we may give an answer to them that sent us. What sayest thou of thyself?

23   He said, I am the voice of one crying in the wilderness, Make straight the way of the Lord, as said the prophet Esaias.

JOHN 3:30

30   He must increase, but I must decrease.

LUKE 1:15

15   For he shall be great in the sight of the Lord, and shall drink neither wine nor strong drink; and he shall be filled with the Holy Ghost, even from his mother's womb.

B. *He had a* _____
_____ . *(vv. 5–6)*

III. A Unique _____ (vv. 7–12)

A. *He was* _____ *for* _____ .
(vv. 7–8)

1 JOHN 4:3

3   And every spirit that confesseth not that Jesus Christ is come in the flesh is not of God: and this is that spirit of antichrist, whereof ye have heard that it should come; and even now already is it in the world.

B. He _____ **their** _____.
(vv. 9–11)

EPHESIANS 2:8–9

8   For by grace are ye saved through faith; and that not of yourselves: it is the gift of God:

9   Not of works, lest any man should boast.

JOHN 1:12–13

12   But as many as received him, to them gave he power to become the sons of God, even to them that believe on his name:

13   Which were born, not of blood, nor of the will of the flesh, nor of the will of man, but of God.

2 TIMOTHY 3:5

5   Having a form of godliness, but denying the power thereof: from such turn away.

C. He _____ **them to** _____.
(vv. 8, 11–12)

ACTS 26:20

20   But shewed first unto them of Damascus, and at Jerusalem, and throughout all the coasts of Judaea, and then to the Gentiles, that they should repent and turn to God, and do works meet for repentance.

Conclusion

_____

_____

_____

TITUS 3:5–6

5 _Not by works of righteousness which we have done, but according to his mercy he saved us, by the washing of regeneration, and renewing of the Holy Ghost;_

6 _Which he shed on us abundantly through Jesus Christ our Saviour;_

1 JOHN 1:8–9

8 _If we say that we have no sin, we deceive ourselves, and the truth is not in us._

9 _If we confess our sins, he is faithful and just to forgive us our sins, and to cleanse us from all unrighteousness._

Study Questions

1. What is the meaning of the word *repentance*?

2. What is the very first thing biblical repentance leads us to?

3. What was the cause of so many people missing John's prophesied identity?

4. Besides his unusual appearance, one of the most notable characteristics of John the Baptist was his humility. What statement did he make in relation to Jesus when his own disciples left him to follow Jesus?

5. Think back to the time you repented of sin and turned to Christ. What has changed in your life as a result?

6. What is the difference between being sorry for sin and actually repenting of sin? Can you think of a time when you have been sorry for something wrong you did, rather than repenting of it?

7. John the Baptist's power was a result of his being filled with the Holy Spirit and his being more in touch with God than he was with the people who were around him. Where do you seek fellowship—with God or with the world? What do you do with the majority of your free time—spend it in activities of the world (watching television, spending time with hobbies, etc.) or in growing in the Lord?

8. Are you seeing fruits of repentance in your own life? How often do you kneel before God in repentance, asking Him for forgiveness and cleansing?

Memory Verse

MATTHEW 3:8

8   *Bring forth therefore fruits meet for repentance:*

Fruits of Compassion

Key Verses

MATTHEW 9:35–38

35 *And Jesus went about all the cities and villages, teaching in their synagogues, and preaching the gospel of the kingdom, and healing every sickness and every disease among the people.*
36 *But when he saw the multitudes, he was moved with compassion on them, because they fainted, and were scattered abroad, as sheep having no shepherd.*
37 *Then saith he unto his disciples, The harvest truly is plenteous, but the labourers are few;*
38 *Pray ye therefore the Lord of the harvest, that he will send forth labourers into his harvest.*

Overview

What is the motivation for the greatest soulwinners and fruit producers? What is one characteristic that when it is absent, it causes us to lose our focus of producing spiritual fruit and when it is present, it spurs us on to greater harvest? The answer—compassion—is deeper than we usually think. Compassion is not simply a sympathetic or even passionate stirring in our hearts when we see or hear of a need in someone's life. Compassion moves us to action. In this lesson, we will learn of Jesus' compassion and the fruit it produced. We will also learn that this fruit-producing compassion is available to us.

Introduction

_____

_____

_____

MARK 10:45

45 For even the Son of man came not to be ministered unto, but to minister, and to give his life a ransom for many.

PHILIPPIANS 2:5–8

5   Let this mind be in you, which was also in Christ Jesus:

6   Who, being in the form of God, thought it not robbery to be equal with God:

7   But made himself of no reputation, and took upon him the form of a servant, and was made in the likeness of men:

8   And being found in fashion as a man, he humbled himself, and became obedient unto death, even the death of the cross.

MATTHEW 9:35

35 And Jesus went about all the cities and villages, teaching in their synagogues, and preaching the gospel of the kingdom, and healing every sickness and every disease among the people.

I. The _____ of Jesus (v. 36)

ISAIAH 53:4–5

4   Surely he hath borne our griefs, and carried our sorrows: yet we did esteem him stricken, smitten of God, and afflicted.

5   But he was wounded for our transgressions, he was bruised for our iniquities: the chastisement of our peace was upon him; and with his stripes we are healed.

A. He was _____. **(v. 36a)**

LAMENTATIONS 3:51

51   Mine eye affecteth mine heart because of all the daughters of my city.

LUKE 19:41–42

41   And when he was come near, he beheld the city, and wept over it,

42   Saying, If thou hadst known, even thou, at least in this thy day, the things which belong unto thy peace! but now they are hid from thine eyes.

B. He was _____. **(v. 36b)**

MARK 2:16–17

16   And when the scribes and Pharisees saw him eat with publicans and sinners, they said unto his disciples, How is it that he eateth and drinketh with publicans and sinners?

17   When Jesus heard it, he saith unto them, They that are whole have no need of the physician, but they that are sick: I came not to call the righteous, but sinners to repentance.

JUDE 22

22   And of some have compassion, making a difference:

II. The _____ of Jesus (v. 37)

A. *There is an* _____.
   (v. 37a)

JOEL 3:11–14

11 Assemble yourselves, and come, all ye heathen, and gather yourselves together round about: thither cause thy mighty ones to come down, O LORD.

12 Let the heathen be wakened, and come up to the valley of Jehoshaphat: for there will I sit to judge all the heathen round about.

13 Put ye in the sickle, for the harvest is ripe: come, get you down; for the press is full, the fats overflow; for their wickedness is great.

14 Multitudes, multitudes in the valley of decision: for the day of the LORD is near in the valley of decision.

JOEL 1:11

11 Be ye ashamed, O ye husbandmen; howl, O ye vinedressers, for the wheat and for the barley; because the harvest of the field is perished.

JEREMIAH 8:20

20 The harvest is past, the summer is ended, and we are not saved.

JOHN 9:4

4 I must work the works of him that sent me, while it is day: the night cometh, when no man can work.

B. There is an _____**.**
   (v. 37b)

1 CORINTHIANS 3:6, 9
6   *I have planted, Apollos watered; but God gave the increase.*
9   *For we are labourers together with God: ye are God's husbandry, ye are God's building.*

PSALM 126:6
6   *He that goeth forth and weepeth, bearing precious seed, shall doubtless come again with rejoicing, bringing his sheaves with him.*

III. The _____ of Jesus (v. 38)

A. It is a commission to _____**. (v. 38a)**

B. It is a commission to _____**. (v. 38b)**

MARK 16:15
15   *And he said unto them, Go ye into all the world, and preach the gospel to every creature.*

LUKE 14:23
23   *And the lord said unto the servant, Go out into the highways and hedges, and compel them to come in, that my house may be filled.*

ACTS 1:8
8   *But ye shall receive power, after that the Holy Ghost is come upon you: and ye shall be witnesses unto me both in*

Jerusalem, and in all Judaea, and in Samaria, and unto the uttermost part of the earth.

Conclusion

_____

_____

_____

JOHN 3:16

16 For God so loved the world, that he gave his only begotten Son, that whosoever believeth in him should not perish, but have everlasting life.

Study Questions

1. What was Jesus' last command while He was on earth?

2. What was Jesus' only prayer request?

3. What are the three phases of every crop, and which phase did Jesus use to describe the harvest of souls?

4. How can we simultaneously share the gospel with those in our community and in the rest of the world?

5. Compassion has been described as "your hurt in my heart." What steps can you take to feel people's hurts to the point that they affect your heart?

6. How does compassion relate to sharing the gospel? Do you have this kind of compassion?

7. For the fruits of compassion to be seen in your life, make a commitment to see people and their needs through Christ's eyes of compassion and to go beyond sympathy to actually meet their needs. Write out a prayer to that effect here, and then keep a record of the differences that seeing people through Christ's eyes of compassion makes in your life throughout this week.

8. Just as you have benefited by Christ's compassion (through forgiveness of sins, peace with God, and a promised future in Heaven), how can you share that same compassion with others who don't know Christ this week?

Memory Verses

MATTHEW 9:37–38

37 Then saith he unto his disciples, The harvest truly is plenteous, but the labourers are few;
38 Pray ye therefore the Lord of the harvest, that he will send forth labourers into his harvest.

Fruits of Biblical Ministry

Key Verses

2 CORINTHIANS 5:14–21

14 For the love of Christ constraineth us; because we thus judge, that if one died for all, then were all dead:

15 And that he died for all, that they which live should not henceforth live unto themselves, but unto him which died for them, and rose again.

16 Wherefore henceforth know we no man after the flesh: yea, though we have known Christ after the flesh, yet now henceforth know we him no more.

17 Therefore if any man be in Christ, he is a new creature: old things are passed away; behold, all things are become new

18 And all things are of God, who hath reconciled us to himself by Jesus Christ, and hath given to us the ministry of reconciliation;

19 To wit, that God was in Christ, reconciling the world unto himself, not imputing their trespasses unto them; and hath committed unto us the word of reconciliation.

20 Now then we are ambassadors for Christ, as though God did beseech you by us: we pray you in Christ's stead, be ye reconciled to God.

21 For he hath made him to be sin for us, who knew no sin; that we might be made the righteousness of God in him.

Overview

Fruit producing requires us to be grounded in ministry, and ministry is a calling for every believer. It takes different forms in various lives, but all biblical ministry must be centered in God's Word. From that rooted center we grow, serve God, share the gospel, minister, and produce fruit. This lesson will examine the motivation behind and the fruit of biblical ministry.

Introduction

_____

_____

_____

2 Corinthians 5:14–15, 18

14 For the love of Christ constraineth us; because we thus judge, that if one died for all, then were all dead:

15 And that he died for all, that they which live should not henceforth live unto themselves, but unto him which died for them, and rose again.

18 And all things are of God, who hath reconciled us to himself by Jesus Christ, and hath given to us the ministry of reconciliation;

I. Rooted in the _____ (vv. 18–19)

A. Scripture is the _____ of God.

1 Corinthians 2:4

4 And my speech and my preaching was not with enticing words of man's wisdom, but in demonstration of the Spirit and of power:

2 Peter 1:21

21 For the prophecy came not in old time by the will of man: but holy men of God spake as they were moved by the Holy Ghost.

2 TIMOTHY 2:15

15   *Study to shew thyself approved unto God, a workman that needeth not to be ashamed, rightly dividing the word of truth.*

JOSHUA 1:8

8   *This book of the law shall not depart out of thy mouth; but thou shalt meditate therein day and night, that thou mayest observe to do according to all that is written therein: for then thou shalt make thy way prosperous, and then thou shalt have good success.*

JAMES 1:22

22   *But be ye doers of the word, and not hearers only, deceiving your own selves.*

B. Scripture is the _____ of ministry.

ACTS 21:19

19   *And when he had saluted them, he declared particularly what things God had wrought among the Gentiles by his ministry.*

ACTS 20:24

24   *But none of these things move me, neither count I my life dear unto myself, so that I might finish my course with joy, and the ministry, which I have received of the Lord Jesus, to testify the gospel of the grace of God.*

ACTS 6:4

4   *But we will give ourselves continually to prayer, and to the ministry of the word.*

EPHESIANS 4:11–12

11 And he gave some, apostles; and some, prophets; and some, evangelists; and some, pastors and teachers;

12 For the perfecting of the saints, for the work of the ministry, for the edifying of the body of Christ:

C. Scripture gives _____ of reconciliation.

2 CORINTHIANS 5:19

19 To wit, that God was in Christ, reconciling the world unto himself, not imputing their trespasses unto them; and hath committed unto us the word of reconciliation.

1 PETER 3:15

15 But sanctify the Lord God in your hearts: and be ready always to give an answer to every man that asketh you a reason of the hope that is in you with meekness and fear:

II. Rooted in _____ (vv. 19–20)

A. Christ has given us a specific _____. (v. 19)

JOHN 20:21

21 Then said Jesus to them again, Peace be unto you: as my Father hath sent me, even so send I you.

MATTHEW 28:19–20

19 Go ye therefore, and teach all nations, baptizing them in the name of the Father, and of the Son, and of the Holy Ghost:

20   *Teaching them to observe all things whatsoever I have commanded you: and, lo, I am with you alway, even unto the end of the world. Amen.*

B.   Christ has given us a privileged _____.
   (v. 20)

2 CORINTHIANS 6:1
1   *We then, as workers together with him, beseech you also that ye receive not the grace of God in vain.*

III. Rooted in the _____ (v. 21)

A.   We are rooted through the _____.

2 CORINTHIANS 5:17
17   *Therefore if any man be in Christ, he is a new creature: old things are passed away; behold, all things are become new.*

ROMANS 1:16
16   *For I am not ashamed of the gospel of Christ: for it is the power of God unto salvation to every one that believeth; to the Jew first, and also to the Greek.*

B.   We are rooted by the _____.

ACTS 1:8
8   *But ye shall receive power, after that the Holy Ghost is come upon you: and ye shall be witnesses unto me both in Jerusalem, and in all Judaea, and in Samaria, and unto the uttermost part of the earth.*

JOHN 3:6

6   That which is born of the flesh is flesh; and that which is born of the Spirit is spirit.

ACTS 4:31

31   And when they had prayed, the place was shaken where they were assembled together; and they were all filled with the Holy Ghost, and they spake the word of God with boldness.

Conclusion

_____

_____

_____

Study Questions

1. What was the motivation behind Paul's great passion to share the gospel?

2. We, like Paul, have a motivating ministry given to us by Jesus (found in 2 Corinthians 5:18). What is that ministry?

3. Name three ways you can become rooted in Scripture.

4. Who does God use to take the message of reconciliation to fallen man?

5. Biblically speaking, what needs to be present for ministry to take place?

6. Do your relationships with young Christians involve fellowship in the Word of God? What can you do this week to make God's Word an integral part of those relationships?

7. What importance do you give to your office as an ambassador for Christ? What steps can you take to enable you to represent Christ more fully and more faithfully?

8. When you have opportunity to share the gospel, do you hesitate in fear? Commit to reminding yourself of the power of the Holy Spirit which is in you—the only power that can really lead a person to salvation. Write down at least two verses from this lesson that you can memorize to remind you that the Holy Spirit's power is available for you.

Memory Verse

2 CORINTHIANS 5:18
18 And all things are of God, who hath reconciled us to himself by Jesus Christ, and hath given to us the ministry of reconciliation;

Fruits of Patience

Key Verses

JAMES 5:7–9

7 Be patient therefore, brethren, unto the coming of the Lord. Behold, the husbandman waiteth for the precious fruit of the earth, and hath long patience for it, until he receive the early and latter rain.

8 Be ye also patient; stablish your hearts: for the coming of the Lord draweth nigh.

9 Grudge not one against another, brethren, lest ye be condemned: behold, the judge standeth before the door.

Overview

Trials and difficulties come to every life, but they do not have to keep us from producing fruit. God instructs us to remain patient through those trials, looking to Christ's soon return. The focus of this lesson is why we should be patient, how we can be patient, and in what areas we are to be patient. And the best part is that God promises fruit to those who are patient!

Introduction

_____

_____

_____

JAMES 5:4–6
4 *Behold, the hire of the labourers who have reaped down your fields, which is of you kept back by fraud, crieth: and the cries of them which have reaped are entered into the ears of the Lord of sabaoth.*
5 *Ye have lived in pleasure on the earth, and been wanton; ye have nourished your hearts, as in a day of slaughter.*
6 *Ye have condemned and killed the just; and he doth not resist you.*

PROVERBS 15:29
29 *The LORD is far from the wicked: but he heareth the prayer of the righteous.*

JOB 5:7
7 *Yet man is born unto trouble, as the sparks fly upward.*

I. The _____ in Harvest (v. 7)

A. *Be patient for His* _____ *. (v. 7a)*

1 THESSALONIANS 2:19
19 *For what is our hope, or joy, or crown of rejoicing? Are not even ye in the presence of our Lord Jesus Christ at his coming?*

MATTHEW 24:27–30

27 For as the lightning cometh out of the east, and shineth even unto the west; so shall also the coming of the Son of man be.

28 For wheresoever the carcase is, there will the eagles be gathered together.

29 Immediately after the tribulation of those days shall the sun be darkened, and the moon shall not give her light, and the stars shall fall from heaven, and the powers of the heavens shall be shaken:

30 And then shall appear the sign of the Son of man in heaven: and then shall all the tribes of the earth mourn, and they shall see the Son of man coming in the clouds of heaven with power and great glory.

1 JOHN 3:3

3 And every man that hath this hope in him purifieth himself, even as he is pure.

B. Be patient in His _____. (v. 7b)

PHILIPPIANS 4:5

5 Let your moderation be known unto all men. The Lord is at hand.

C. Be patient for His _____. (v. 7c)

GALATIANS 6:9

9 And let us not be weary in well doing: for in due season we shall reap, if we faint not.

PSALM 1:3

3   And he shall be like a tree planted by the rivers of water, that bringeth forth his fruit in his season; his leaf also shall not wither; and whatsoever he doeth shall prosper.

TITUS 2:13

13   Looking for that blessed hope, and the glorious appearing of the great God and our Saviour Jesus Christ;

II. The _____ for the Harvest (v. 8)

A. We must have _____ hearts. (v. 8a)

PSALM 55:22

22   Cast thy burden upon the LORD, and he shall sustain thee: he shall never suffer the righteous to be moved.

1 CORINTHIANS 15:58

58   Therefore, my beloved brethren, be ye stedfast, unmoveable, always abounding in the work of the Lord, forasmuch as ye know that your labour is not in vain in the Lord.

ACTS 2:42

42   And they continued stedfastly in the apostles' doctrine and fellowship, and in breaking of bread, and in prayers.

HEBREWS 10:23–25

23   Let us hold fast the profession of our faith without wavering; (for he is faithful that promised;)

24 And let us consider one another to provoke unto love and to good works:

25 Not forsaking the assembling of ourselves together, as the manner of some is; but exhorting one another: and so much the more, as ye see the day approaching.

TITUS 1:9

9 Holding fast the faithful word as he hath been taught, that he may be able by sound doctrine both to exhort and to convince the gainsayers.

EPHESIANS 3:16

16 That he would grant you, according to the riches of his glory, to be strengthened with might by his Spirit in the inner man;

B. We must have _____ hearts. (v. 8b)

1 PETER 1:3–4

3 Blessed be the God and Father of our Lord Jesus Christ, which according to his abundant mercy hath begotten us again unto a lively hope by the resurrection of Jesus Christ from the dead,

4 To an inheritance incorruptible, and undefiled, and that fadeth not away, reserved in heaven for you,

III. The _____ of the Harvest (v. 9)

A. Be at peace with _____. (v. 9a)

EPHESIANS 4:1–3, 30–32

1   *I therefore, the prisoner of the Lord, beseech you that ye walk worthy of the vocation wherewith ye are called,*

2   *With all lowliness and meekness, with longsuffering, forbearing one another in love;*

3   *Endeavouring to keep the unity of the Spirit in the bond of peace.*

30   *And grieve not the holy Spirit of God, whereby ye are sealed unto the day of redemption.*

31   *Let all bitterness, and wrath, and anger, and clamour, and evil speaking, be put away from you, with all malice:*

32   *And be ye kind one to another, tenderhearted, forgiving one another, even as God for Christ's sake hath forgiven you.*

B. *Be aware of the* _____ . *(v. 9b)*

REVELATION 20:11–12

11   *And I saw a great white throne, and him that sat on it, from whose face the earth and the heaven fled away; and there was found no place for them.*

12   *And I saw the dead, small and great, stand before God; and the books were opened: and another book was opened, which is the book of life: and the dead were judged out of those things which were written in the books, according to their works.*

MATTHEW 7:1

1   *Judge not, that ye be not judged.*

2 CORINTHIANS 5:10

10   *For we must all appear before the judgment seat of Christ; that every one may receive the things done in his*

body, according to that he hath done, whether it be good or bad.

1 CORINTHIANS 4:5

5   *Therefore judge nothing before the time, until the Lord come, who both will bring to light the hidden things of darkness, and will make manifest the counsels of the hearts: and then shall every man have praise of God.*

Conclusion

_____

_____

_____

Study Questions

1. What is the Christian's stabilizing hope in trouble?

2. In what three areas does our text say that troubled Christians should direct their anticipation and hope to?

3. Describe the two seasons of rain—the early and latter rain.

4. In what two ways should we live in light of Christ's coming according to this lesson?

5. What personal burdens or trials have you thought of throughout this lesson that you need to be patient in and remind yourself of Christ's presence and His coming?

6. Scripture instructs us to look forward to Christ's coming with patience, but we have a job to do as we wait. In what areas of ministry are you currently serving Christ? What areas, if any, has He convicted you of that you have not followed through on? What steps can you take this week to begin following Him in those areas?

7. God promises us that we will reap if we faint not. Are there areas in which you have fainted? What can you do to re-establish your footing in those areas?

8. Bitterness and anger keep us from producing spiritual fruit. Is there anyone you are not at peace with? What steps can you take toward true reconciliation?

Memory Verse

James 5:8

8 *Be ye also patient; stablish your hearts: for the coming of the Lord draweth nigh.*

For additional Christian
growth resources visit
www.strivingtogether.com